This book
belongs to a girl
who has girl power: you!

_____

(your name here)

Titles by Ashley Rice
Published by
Blue Mountain Arts®

For an Incredible Kid
Girls Rule
Sisters Are Forever Friends
You Are a Girl Who Can Do Anything
You Are a Girl Who Totally Rocks!

For an Incredible Girl/Para una niña increíble
(Bilingual Edition)

Library of Congress Control Number: 2013937878
ISBN: 978-1-59842-755-4

◪ and Blue Mountain Press are registered in U.S. Patent and Trademark Office.
Certain trademarks are used under license.

Printed in China.
Fifth Printing: 2016

Blue Mountain Arts, Inc.
P.O. Box 4549, Boulder, Colorado 80306

Use Your
Girl
Power

Nothing Can
Hold You Back!

Ashley Rice

Blue Mountain Press™
Boulder, Colorado

Use Your Girl Power to change the World

There are girls who make things better...
simply by showing up.
There are girls who make things happen,
girls who make their way.
There are girls who make a difference,
girls who make us smile.
There are girls who do not make excuses,
girls who cannot be replaced.
There are girls of wit and wisdom who –
with strength and courage –
make it through...
There are girls who use their girl power
to change the world every day...
girls like YOU.

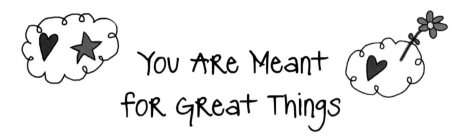

You Are Meant for Great Things

Believe in **yourself** and all you want to be. Don't let what other people say or do make you frown. **Laugh** as much as possible. Let in the **good times** and get through the bad. Be **happy** with who and where you are. You are in the **right place**, and your heart is leading you to a great **tomorrow**.

When circumstances seem difficult, **pull through** them. This will make you stronger than you think. The longer you **practice** the habit of working toward your dreams, the easier the **journey** will become.

You are meant for **great** things.

With the Girl Power in You...

There's no telling what you can do. Concentrate on learning... concentrate on courage. TRY a different way, or learn a little more. Set goals and then stick with them. When you fall down, get up again. Believe in what you do and who you are... and you'll go far.

Always Remember that...

You Totally Rock!

Don't Let Anything Hold You Back

If **anyone** tries to tell you that you can't work hard enough to **face** the task in front of you — show them you're **tough**. If anyone tries to tell you that you are not that strong, don't listen to discouragement — **know** that you belong.

If anyone tries to tell you that you can't **sing** your own song **OR** make your way in the world...

prove them **wrong**.

Having Girl Power Means...

being **brave**

being athletic

being intelligent

being fabulous

being super

being funny...

...but mostly it means
being you...

...and the combination of traits,
talents, and personal
qualities that make you who
you are!

Always Be
True to You

Being **true** to yourself can be scary.
First, you've got to face **everything**
around you and figure out what is
important: what you **think** really counts.
Second, you've got to **interact** with a lot
of people who may see things differently.
But life has lots of **smiles** and frowns, as
days have their own **ups** and downs.

If you **aRe** true to yourself in all that you do, and if you keep **working** to make your dReams come true... then you will achieve success just by doing your **best**.

You've got everything it **takes** to be true to you.

You Are an Amazing Girl

Amazing girls are discoverers of new paths. Amazing girls are trailblazers and superheroines and confidantes. Amazing girls have courage, strength, humor, and love. Amazing girls know how to laugh and to listen, to dare and to try. Amazing girls don't give up when the going gets tough.

Amazing girls are students
and seekers, learners and keepers
of goals and dreams and of the
unexpected. Amazing girls believe in
themselves and reach for the stars.
Amazing girls are daughters and
sisters and friends.

You are an amazing
girl.

Embrace What Makes You Unique

Be **happy** with what you have.
What you've **got** is more
than what you need
to get through **each day**.
Appreciate your creativity,
your mindfulness,
and your **ability** to **encourage** others
when situations are hard.

Be glad of who you are today,
for you have **so much** to offer
to yourself and to those around **you**.
You are a **fighter** and a dreamer,
an inventor of fun things,
and a **girl** who has so much
to **give** to this world!

There Is Only One You

You have your
very own ways.

You've got your own
walking shoes.

You are the
only one who
smiles and laughs
exactly as you do.

You are the
only one who lives
and thinks exactly
as you do.

You are your
very own you.

You've got your
own dreams and
your ideas too...
There is only one
you.

Being a Girl in the World Is a Wonderful Thing

Being a girl in the **world**
is a **wonderful** thing.
You can do most anything
you put your **mind** to.
You can **write** a book.
You can start a band.
You can become a **doctor**.
You can dream and plan.
You can handle adversity.
You can **stand** up tall.
And in all these things,
you are **beautiful**.
You are strong.
Being a **girl** in the world
is a wonderful thing.
You **can** do most **anything**
you put your mind to.

It Takes Guts

It takes guts to **dream** big dreams.
It takes guts to be who you are.
It takes guts to see big things:
to learn, to grow, and —
knowing what you know —
to move forward in the direction
of your dreams.
It takes guts to dream these dreams.
It takes guts to stay who you are.

"Guts," of course, is just
another name for
girl power.
And without it
we would never
reach the stars.

Girl, you've
got guts.

YOU:

The **words** you say...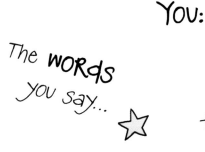

the **friends** you make...

the **stuff** you know...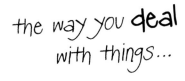

the **Risks** you take...

the way you **deal** with things...

and the **life** you make every day...

These are **all**
parts of what
make you so
great.

Things You Should Know

1. It's impossible to be perfect all the time, and it's okay to make mistakes — they're part of what helps you learn, and they make you who you are.

2. In part, at least, you make your own luck: the more doors you try, the more doors or opportunities will open up for you and the more chances will come your way.

And (most importantly)...

3. You're doing an
   awesome job!

You're Headed in the Right Direction

Take **note** of all the good
you have done in the **past**,
and always celebrate
your **accomplishments**.
Sometimes no one
is going to **tell** you
that you are doing a **good** job
except yourself.
So tell yourself that!
It's important to concentrate
on the **direction**
you are going in
and to believe **with** all your heart
that you can get **there**.

Don't worry **too** much
if you stumble or fall.
There is **always** time
to make up for your mistakes
and to press on
toward a **great** future.
If you find things difficult,
reflect on **where** you are
and where you want to **go**.
Be mindful of everything
around you and how it
influences your **life** every day.
You are in the **right** place,
and there's **nothing**
you can't achieve
if you **really** go for it!

How to Get to Your Future

1. WORK hard

2. Study hard

3. Learn as much as possible

4. Laugh

5. Have fun

6. Make your future your own

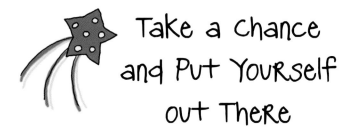

Take a Chance and Put Yourself out There

Be **grateful** for the gifts
you have been given,
and **use** them
to your greatest ability!
Follow the light that was meant
for **you** and you alone.
There is **beauty** to be
found everywhere —
you just have to **look** for it
and let it into your life
whenever you **find** it.
It **will** lead you on
to great **discoveries** about yourself
and the world around you.

Do not **be** afraid to take a chance,
put yourself **out** there,
and take a **step**
in the right direction.
There is a **world** of possibilities
just **waiting** for you
to uncover them.
Make **friends** with yourself,
and be the best friend
you **can** be to others.
Embrace this life
with all of the **spirit**
that you can, and you will
experience the happiness
you've **always** dreamed of.

Never, Never, Never Give Up

Don't give up
when the cards
are stacked
against you
and hope
seems hard to find.
DON'T give up,
don't give in,
and don't give up
the fight.

Never surrender —
even when something
stands in your way.
There are stars to find
and mountains to climb,
and you'll get there one day.

What If?

What would have happened if **Amelia Earhart** had never gotten on a plane? What if **Rosa Parks** had decided not to make a stand on that bus? What if **Harriet Tubman** had been too scared to pioneer the Underground Railroad or if your **favorite** female novelist had decided writing was too risky or too **hard**?

What if all these amazing women had decided not to **step out** from the crowd, decided not to take any **chances**? All of their achievements would be lost to us. Instead, they chose to give people **hope** and to fight for change.

What if **you** took a chance, gave it your all, **stood up** for something you believed in? There's no telling what you might do!

I believe!

You **belong** to a long line
of women who began as
girls dReaming —
and gRew up
Keeping on believing —
and gRew up to **be**
women of intellect, couRage,
vision, and cReativity...

...women who make
a difference.

And you are well
on your way
to becoming
one such woman.

There Is Greatness Within You

There are **paths** to greatness that are easy to find, but once you get on them **and** start traveling, you must look **deep** inside your **heart** to figure out the best way to go.

When **searching** for the great role that you will play in this world, you've got to give it your **all** and then some more! There are easier roads to travel, **but** only the roads that **lead** to greatness of heart and mind can give you the **satisfaction** and happiness that you are seeking within your soul.

BReathe deep and look inside youRself, and you will discover the Right **steps** to **lead** you wheRe you Really want to go. You've got **everything** it takes to be gReat!

How to be a ROCK STAR, prizewinner, teacher, astrophysicist, novelist, professional wrestler, actor, painter, radio personality, editor, filmmaker, mathematician, guitar player, columnist, astronaut, singer, designer, cartoonist, inventor, doctor, architect, builder, PRODUCER, writer, athlete, artist, programmer, dancer, technician, or stylist in just one step...

Go for it!

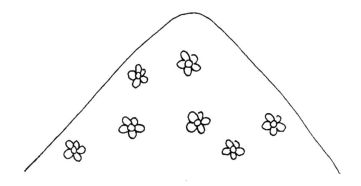

When the task at hand is a **mountain**
in front of you,
it may seem too hard to climb.
But you don't have to **climb** it
all at once —
just one **step** at a time.
Take one **small** step...
and one small step...
then another...
and you'll find...
the task at hand that was a mountain
in front of you...
is a mountain **you** have climbed.

Imagine in your head the story of a very brave person who is **capable**, brilliant, and talented. In front of that person stands a very large mountain. She **must** climb this mountain in order to reach her **goal** — the valley of dreams that lies just on the other **side**. See that person approach the mountain? She is **all** determination. She has overcome similar obstacles before. **Watch** her now as she begins to climb. This is **YOUR** story. It is you against that mountain now. **Go** find your valley of dreams.

Having a Positive Attitude Is Everything

If you **think** you **can** do something, you will be able to complete the task or achieve your specific dreams or goals. Things may not always turn out exactly as you had expected, but with a little work and a little determination and a lot of girl power...

Nothing can hold you back!

A Poem About Daring and Trying

FOR everyone who wants
to sing...
or everyone who wants
to dream...
and everyone who wants
to spin...
and everyone who wants
to win...
for everyone who wants
to dare...
and everyone who wants to
bring forth greatness
in their lives...

Keep going!

On Facing the Competition

These days, competition is fierce. It seems that there are more and more talented people everywhere competing for the same place in the sun, the same patch of sky. However, there are three important things to remember when thinking about facing the competition.

The first thing is to forget the competition because — whatever you're doing — you are always, in the long run, really competing against yourself. In other words... it doesn't matter so much if you get 1st place or 3rd place. What really matters — in regard to what you believe you can do and what you have done in the past — is your own personal "time"...

The **second** thing to Remember when facing the competition is that everyone else feels pretty much the same **way** you do: everyone else — though they may be competing against you in the actual Race — is also trying to beat their **own time**.

And **third**, we can **learn** stuff from the people who are faster than we are, and we can make **friends** with the people who **Run** with us.

We can **figure out** ways to deal with our limitations in the process of competition, and thus find ways around those limitations. **Competition** often **pushes** us to work harder than we might work if we were left completely to our own devices.

No matter what you like to do or what **goals** you pursue, competition is a part of life and will most likely touch your **life** in some way.

Learn from Your Mistakes

As you get older, facing up to the consequences of your actions is a big part of growing up. If you make a mistake, don't be afraid to tell someone or to ask for help or advice. This is the best way to learn from your actions...

...and to keep on growing
up strong.

Who Cares What Other People Think!

DON'T worry too much
about what **others** think about you.
Just do your best **every day**
to reach your hopes and dreams.
Other people have their **own** worries,
their own prejudices,
and their own **lives** to think about,
and they aren't really paying
that much **attention**
to what you are doing
all the **time** anyway.
Whatever the case may be,
don't **ever** let any other
person's words **bother** you.

Stay positive in **all** things,
and **always** look on the bright side.
Your happiness is
in your own hands,
and it's up to you
to **make** your life turn out
as great as you **know** it can be.

Remember to...

Ask questions...
and get advice when you
feel you need it...

Seek out people you admire —
whether in books or in your own life —
and try to learn from them...

Have fun with your interests
and activities...

Give everything your
best shot...

...and don't forget to give yourself a pat on the back every once in a while — you deserve it!

If you are not sure
which way to go...
ask your **heart** –
your heart will **know.**
When your mind
does not know what to **say**...
your heart will
find a way...

When you can't **see**
the finish line
or when your **dreams**
seem hard to find...

Know that **you**
know the way:
your **heart** will
lead you there
one day.

Do not be afraid to
be YOUR true self and
to show the world
all you can be.

The power to be oneself is perhaps one of the best gifts a person can  both "have" and — at the same time — give. It is when we are our true selves that we find our best friends, write our best lines, and score the most points on the never-ending tests that are eternally placed before us...

It is when we are our **true** selves that we discover things we have in common with others... by way of an empathetic **smile** in response to something we've just said or by **running** into others on the path that we've chosen... just because they, too, in being **themselves** and following their hearts, have **chosen** the same **path**. It is when we are true to ourselves that we shine the **brightest**, laugh the loudest, and learn the most.

Being **oneself** often includes **times** we have to run ahead or wait behind... It's when we are ourselves that we can pass off courage to **another** person. This is the "**gift**" part and the reason why being oneself is never a selfish **act**, but one that is rooted — always, **always** — in love, **friendship**, and courage.

You Gotta Have Hope

You gotta keep trying
and you gotta keep believing
that everything you are
striving for and trying to do
is worth something...
And you gotta have some heart
and you gotta have drive...
but mostly you gotta have hope...

...and hope comes from inside.

Trust in Yourself
No Matter What

Choose friends who **value** you
for who you are.
Don't ever sell **yourself** short —
always keep reaching
for that dream.
Trust in yourself to find the answers.
You've got them **inside**
your very own heart.
Don't let **other** people
overinfluence you.
Listen to what others have to say,
but take it **with** a grain of salt
and **do** what you know
you really need to do.
Rely on yourself
to **face** challenges.

Let **go** of the past,
and live up to the **future**.
It's in your own hands.
Stand **up** to change,
and let it transform you

into a **better** person.
celebrate everything
about you that
makes you **so** special,
and always believe
in yourself
to do **what's** right.

You've Got So Much Going for You

You've got so much
to look forward to,
and so many
exciting adventures
lie before you.
Unseen roads await
your footsteps.
Unexplored territories
await your gaze.
You've got so much
going for you.
This is your time
to shine.

Gather together
your courage
and your confidence,
and step out there
and greet the day
with open arms.
There is nothing
but the best
in your future,
and it's all
about to happen.

Let Your Light Shine

Don't be afraid
to go out there
and show the world
all that you've got.
Don't be afraid
to take your place
in the sunshine.
You've done a great job
and you've earned
everything that's
coming to you.

You are **bRave** and tRue
and couRageous and **stRong**.
You deseRve the **best** in life.
So show youR tRue coloRs.
Step out **into** the **light**
and shine!

...and **flower** POWER!

Change Begins
with a Dream

The Road to any Real change or **accomplishment** begins with a dream dreamed by one such as _you_. You may spend too long with your head in a book or a **song** in your head... but you look for the good in everything. You may **believe** too much. You may be a dreamer... and some people might say you should be more **practical**...

...but practically every
idea — every act, **big**
or **small** — gets
its start from a
dream that **begins**
in the **heart,**
like a song.

As You Make Your Way in This World...

Remember to take care of yourself.
Know you are an outstanding person
capable of doing great things.
Accept yourself for who you are,
and don't worry about
the judgments of your peers;
only you know what's best
for you and your dreams.
Walk confidently in the
direction of your hopes
and ambitions.

Remember that greatness lies within you,
but most of all, trust that you can
pull through any situation
with shining colors.
Always believe in yourself,
and never forget who you are.

You Are a Very Special Person

You are **someone**
with many **gifts**
and many dreams.
You have a very
special **heart**
and a very special
way of **being** yourself.

Nothing can compare
to your **spirit**,
your style,
your **smile**,
your laughter.

you are so
special

This is your guardian angel saying that even if things seem a little bit crazy where you are right now, from up here you look pretty good... That tangled mess that's got you worried — it's just a dark cloud...

...and there's a Rainbow
on the OtHeR side.

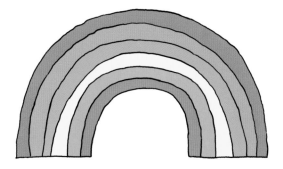

It's not about how well
you **do**...
it's about how hard
you **try** and what kind
of person you are.
There are **many**
things we go through,
and there are many things
we will **triumph** over.
And there will be **times**
when you'll fall down.

But there will be more
times when you
pull through.
And you will find
greatness in your life.
And you will keep getting
stronger every second
of it.

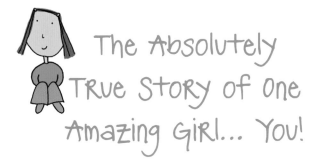

The Absolutely True Story of One Amazing Girl... You!

Once there was a girl... and she was unique and talented and interesting and amazing and unforgettable... and Real. And she knew, deep down, that if she tried something and things didn't go as she had hoped or wanted or dreamed or planned, she could just try something different or try the exact same thing again but approach it in a new or different way. Then, one day, her greatest hopes and dreams actually became true.

And so her life was full of all these amazing and unforgettable moments and events and circumstances: incredible wins, of course, but also equally incredible – and worth it – losses.

Because no matter what happened, she learned from everything around her and everything she went through. Yes, she fell sometimes (like everybody else does), but she got up and moved forward by always being true to herself.

And maybe one day she will even make a path for others to follow... until they can make their own paths too.

You see, it's not that she was never frightened or sad or even knew when she woke up each day what to do (no one does). It was simply that she believed in herself and always shined on like a star. Just like you.

Like a **Rainbow**, you bring color to ordinary places. Like a **sunset**, you add brilliance. Like a River, you know the way. With the patience of the **forests**, you **wait** for your dreams to grow. And like the most special flower in the **garden**...

...you **gRow**
stRongeR and
moRe beautiful
eveRy day.

Keep looking forward to the future...
to all you might be. Don't let old mistakes
or misfortunes hold you down: learn
from them, forgive yourself... or others...
and move on. Do not be bothered or
discouraged by adversity. Instead, meet
it as a challenge. Be empowered by
the courage it takes you to overcome
obstacles. Learn something new every
day. Be interested in others and what
they might teach you. But do not look
for yourself in the faces of others.
Do not look for who you are in other
people's approval.

As far as who you are and who you will become goes — the **answer** is always within yourself. **Believe** in yourself. Follow your heart and your dreams. You... like everyone... will make mistakes. But so long as you are **true** to the strength within your own heart... you can never go wrong.

In This World,
Wishing You...

a little peace

a little **love**

a little luck

a little sunshine

a little **happiness**

a little fun...

...and as far
as changing
the **WORLD**?

You can **do** it!

You are a very special star...

Go on and shine,
go on and shine,
go on and
shine.